Windswept,
 Thank you for having us. We love it here!
 ♡ Megan Levy

This book is dedicated to Mother Earth, to Liam, and to Max, who is no longer with us Earth-side.

This is a work of fiction. Names, characters, places, and incidents are the product of the author's imagination.

Copyright © 2021 by Megan Lynn Levy

All rights reserved. No part of this book may be reproduced or used in any manner without written permission of the copyright owner except for the use of quotations in a book review. For more information, address: megan@unmaskedmotherhood.com

First edition November 2021

Book design and Illustrations by Tara Victoria

ISBN: 978-1-7378302-0-7 (hardcover)

Printed in China. Guangzhou Bonroy Cultural Creativity Co., Ltd
No.3 Kangmei Road, Fuling Industry Park, Tangmei, Xintang Town, Zengcheng, Guangzhou China 511340

www.unmaskedmotherhood.com

WE SHELL FLIP

A SPECIAL TALE FOR CHILDREN AND CAREGIVERS

BY MEGAN LYNN LEVY

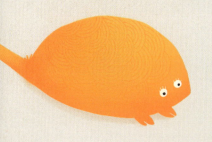

ILLUSTRATED BY
TARA VICTORIA

 When you see this icon, flip the book!

"Good Morning, World!"

Helen, a horseshoe crab, wrote with her long, colorful tail as the ocean waves sparkled.

It was supposed to be another wonderful day.

Helen and her parents were about to start their beach dance.

Whoosh!

A strong wind blew.
It pushed Helen onto her back.

Flip the book!

But her world still looked different.

Helen squinted and batted her eyelashes.

She kicked and wiggled her bendy legs. But she remained upside down.

"Oh no!" Helen cried, "I'm stuck! The world is upside down."

She remembered that writing with her tail always made her feel better.

Helen closed her eyes.

Whoosh!

A strong wind blew Helen's note down to the shoreline toward the ocean.

Helen sketched a note onto a nearby newspaper clipping.

"*Dear Mommy and Daddy. I feel sad. I wish I could flip back over.*"

Mommy and Daddy unraveled the note. But it was wet and they couldn't make out what it said!

Helen's Mommy sensed something was wrong.

"*Let's look for Helen!*" she said.

Her parents scooted and slid Helen back down the hill toward the shoreline.

Flip the book!

Up the sandhill they went . . .

And there was Helen flipped
onto her back!

"Helen!" said Mommy, *"We're
here to help!"*

"I can. I will. I shell..."

"Okay!" said Helen, "Let me try!"

"We can. We will. We shall flip, together!"

"Like this," they said.

Then Mommy and Daddy showed her how to flip over.

Help Helen flip over! Flip the book!

"...flip!"

Plop!

Everything looked right again!

Helen's tears dried and she smiled. She knew that writing would be her superpower forever.

Knowing they would always have her back, Helen and her family danced in the moonlight.